THIS CANDLEWICK BOOK BELONGS TO:

_____

_____

_____

_____

First U.S. paperback edition in this form 1996
First published individually in Great Britain as *John Burningham's Colors,*
John Burningham's Opposites, John Burningham's a b c, and *John Burningham's 1 2 3*
in 1985 by Walker Books Ltd., London

Library of Congress Cataloging-in-Publication Data

Burningham, John.
First steps: letters, numbers, colors, opposites / John Burningham.—1st U.S. ed.
"First published as John Burningham's colors,
John Burningham's opposites, John Burningham's a b c, and John Burningham's 1 2 3
in 1985 by Walker Books Ltd., London."
Summary: An illustrated introduction to the letters of the alphabet,
the numbers one to ten, basic colors, and opposites.
ISBN 1-56402-205-6 (hardcover)—ISBN 1-56402-598-5 (paperback)
[1. Alphabet. 2. Counting. 3. Colors.
4. English language—Synonyms and antonyms.] I. Title.
PZ7.B936Fi   1993
[E]—dc20   93-18844

2 4 6 8 10 9 7 5 3 1

Printed in Hong Kong

The pictures in this book were done in
colored inks and colored pencils.

Candlewick Press
2067 Massachusetts Avenue
Cambridge, Massachusetts 02140

JOHN BURNINGHAM

First Steps

Letters Numbers Colors Opposites

CANDLEWICK PRESS
CAMBRIDGE, MASSACHUSETTS

Letters

a
alligator

b
bear

c
cow

d
duck

e
elephant

f
flowers

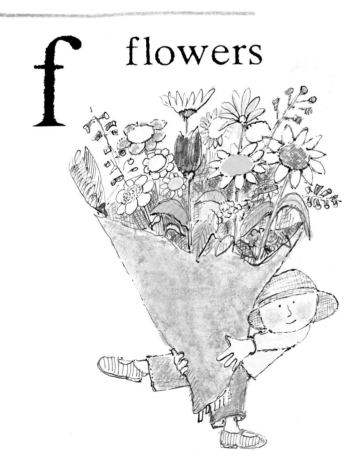

g goat

h hippopotamus

i
ice cream

j juggler

k kangaroo

l
lion

m monkey

n newt

o ostrich

p parrot

q queen

r rabbit

s snake

t
turtle

u
umbrella

V
violin

W
wasp

x xylophone

y
yak

z zebra

Numbers

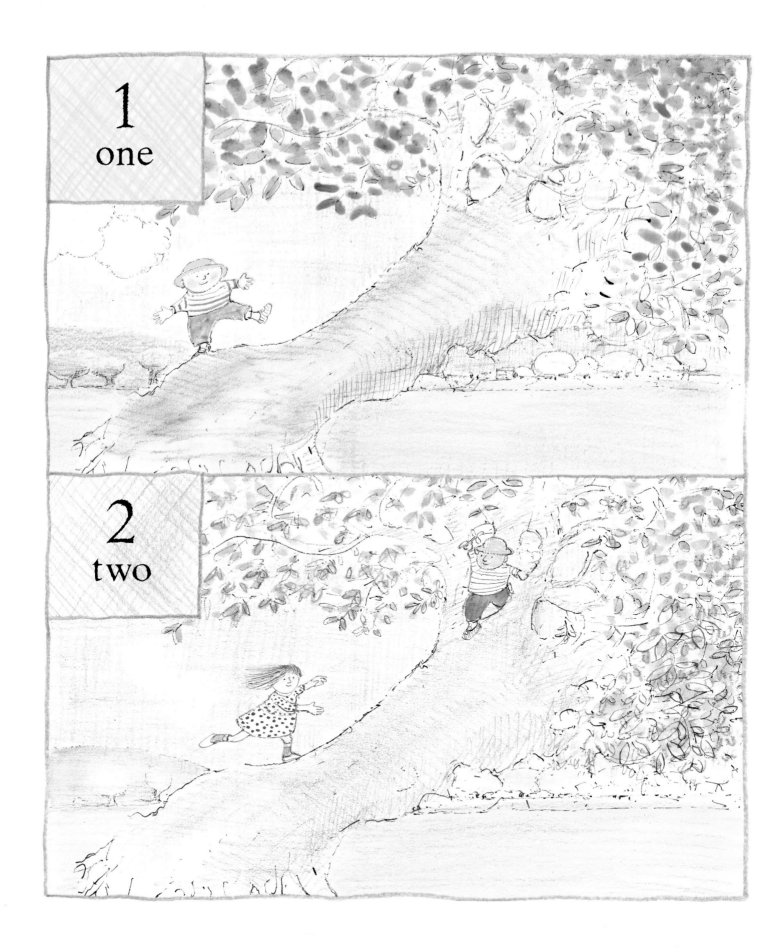

1 one

2 two

3 three

4 four

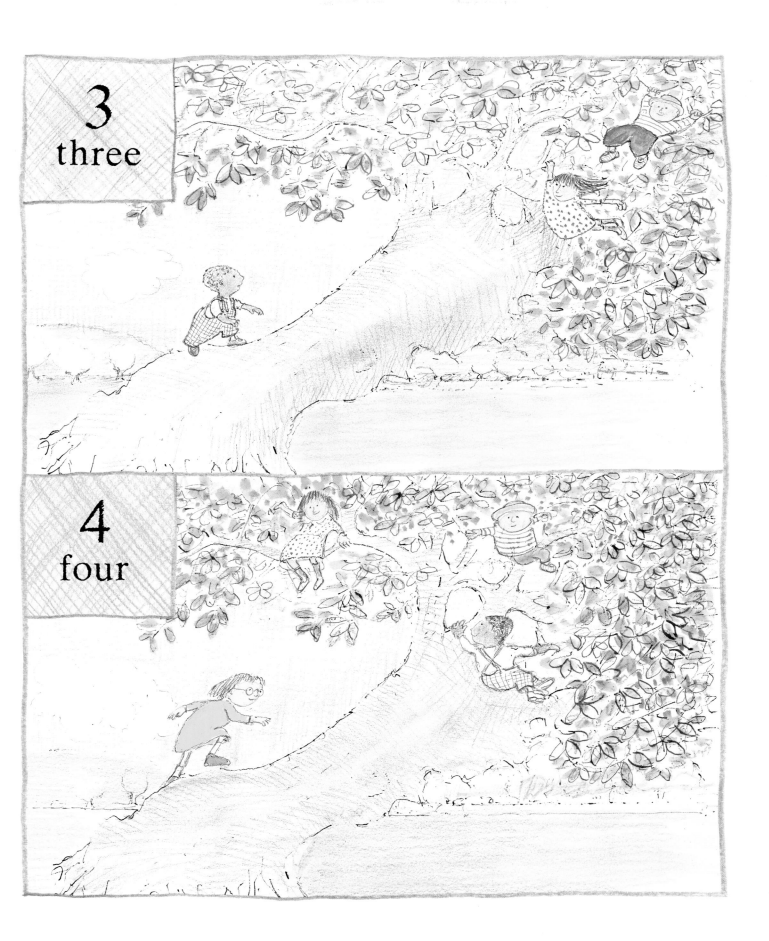

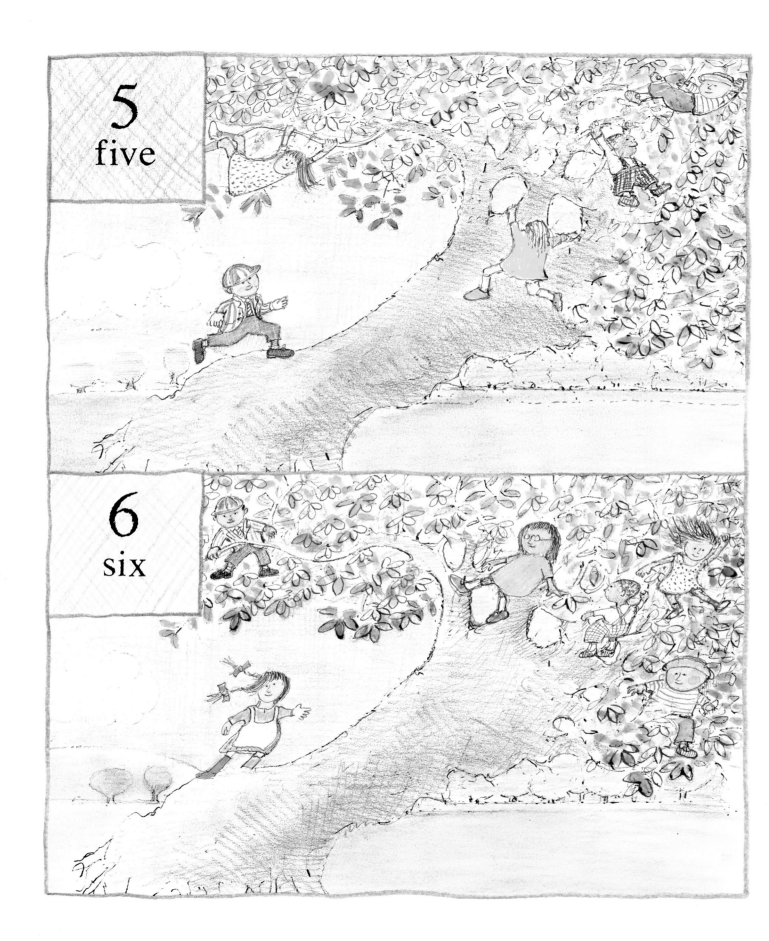

5
five

6
six

7
seven

8
eight

9
nine

10
ten

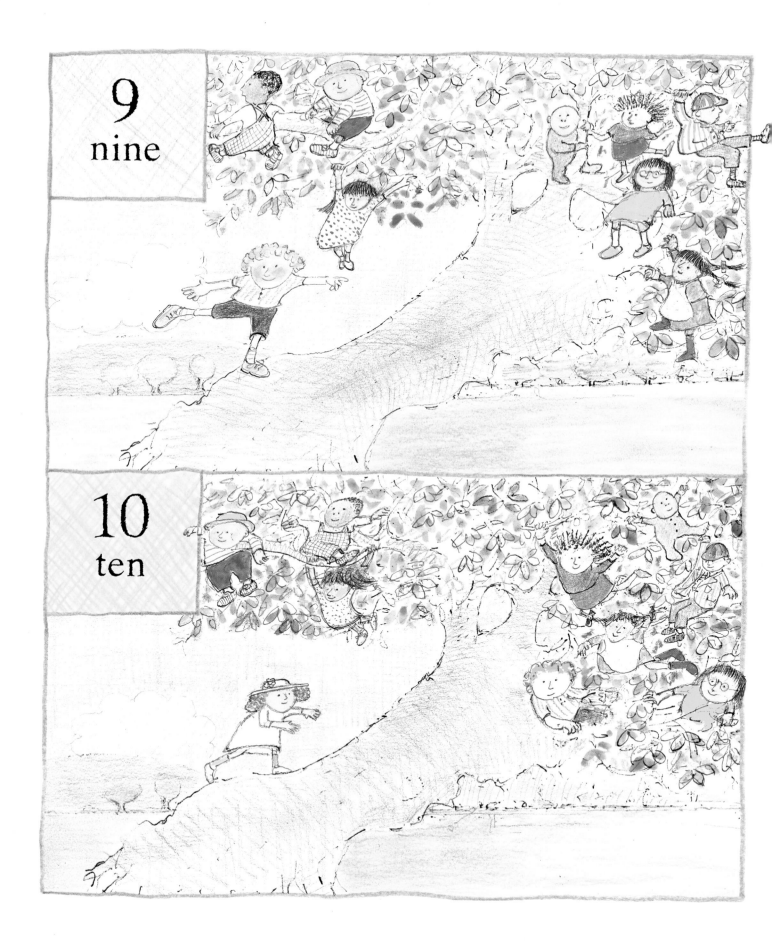

Colors

red

yellow

blue

purple

orange

green

white

black

red

yellow

blue

purple

orange

green

white

black

Opposites

dry

wet

hard

soft

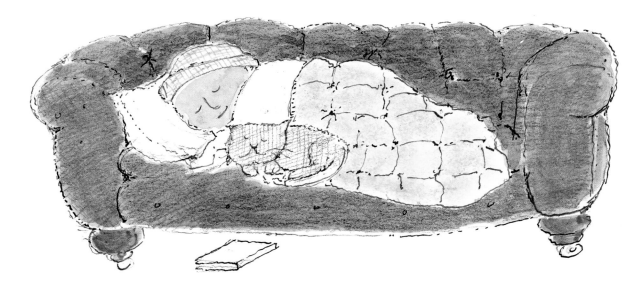

light

heavy

noisy

quiet

hot

cold

slow

fast

young

old

big

little

thin

fat

push

pull

open

shut

JOHN BURNINGHAM is one of the most successful author-illustrators of his time. He has written and illustrated many highly acclaimed children's books, including *Mr. Gumpy's Outing; Aldo; Hey! Get Off Our Train; Harvey Slumfenburger's Christmas Present;* and *The Dog, The Friend, The Blanket,* and *The Baby.* About *First Steps* he says, "If you can make learning interesting and amusing, then you're off on the right foot." John Burningham is a three-time winner of *The New York Times* Best Illustrated Children's Book of the Year Award and a two-time winner of the Kate Greenaway Medal, as well as a recipient of the *Boston Globe–Horn Book* Award.